The Gift Of Words

William Benedict

TEACH Services, Inc.
P U B L I S H I N G
www.TEACHServices.com • (800) 367-1844

All rights reserved. No part of this publication may be reproduced, distributed, or transmitted in any form or by any means, including photocopying, recording, or other electronic or mechanical methods, without the prior written permission of the publisher, except in the case of brief quotations embodied in critical reviews and certain other noncommercial uses permitted by copyright law. For permission requests, write to the publisher, TEACH Services, Inc., at the address below.

The author assumes full responsibility for the accuracy of all facts and quotations as cited in this book.

Copyright © 2021 William Benedict
Copyright © 2021 TEACH Services, Inc.
ISBN-13: 978-1-4796-1391-5 (Paperback)
ISBN-13: 978-1-4796-1392-2 (ePub)
Library of Congress Control Number: 2021909480

Scripture taken from the New American Standard Bible, Copyright © 1960, 1962, 1963, 1968, 1971, 1972, 1973, 1975, 1977 by the Lockman Foundation. Used by permission.

Published by

www.TEACHServices.com • (800) 367-1844

When the God of Israel

undertakes work

for us

He will make it

a success,

Sons and Daughters of God, p. 278

I would like my words

to rest in the minds and hearts of those

that hear and read.

William Benedict

TO SEE

BEAUTY

GOODNESS

EACH DAY

LOVE

Table of Contents

Is Love 13

This World 14

You 16

We Cannot 17

There Is 18

When 19

Please 20

A Fool 21

Spring 22

Silence 23

To Say 24

Time 25

Did Love 26

Over 27

Let 28

Taste 29

As I 30

Who 31

Images	32
Such Love	33
To See	34
The Sun	35
Within	36
His Hands	37
To Be	38
To Wait	39
Wear	40
A Life	41
Light	42
The Peace	43
Such	44
Winter	45
Come	46
Memories	47
Always	48
Giving	49
Star	50
Before	51
Tears	52
Life	53
Now When	54
A Wish	56

Hush	57
If	58
How Much	59
Welcome	60
One	61
Prayer	62
Reasons	63
A Spring	64
Why	65
Lord	66
Fill	67
Cover	68
Jesus Love	70
I Had	71
Since	72
I Walk	73
Choose	74
Worry	75
Who Can	76
Will One	77
Plead	78
Walking	79
A Way	80
It Matters	82

Friend	83
Ever	84
Valley	85
Passing	86
Stop	88
Words	89
Love	90
Be	91
Getting Old	92
Since	93
Joy	94
Lord	95
Is On	96
Hear	97
Why	98
How Much	99
Moments	100
Destiny	101
A Friend	102
The Love Encounter	103
Depths of Love	104
Prisoner of Love	105
In Uncertain Times	106
This Is My Life	107

Remember	108
In the Presence of Time	110
The Legend	111
By the River	112
Have You Heard Spring Come	113
Counting the Gain	114
The Path Today	115
Steps Today	116
Freedom Nine-Eleven	117
If Only	118
Taste And See	119
A Place In Time	120
Spring	121
Oh Spring	122
I Sing	123
The Stillness	124
Freedom's March	125
Thankful	126
A Place in Time	128

Is Love

Love is a mountain
higher than,
I can climb,
harder to find,
as visions,
in the night.

Love permeates
the being,
as magic,
in time.

The mountain,
still seems
high.

Forthright
in bestowals,
shadows sublime.

The mountain
still seems high,
the darkness night.

Where is my
companion,
as the wind
flees,
long and far.

Oh, where,
do you keep,
the warm and
tenderness,
that seems to hide,
in love and peace?

William Benedict

This World

This world is not all
sorrow and misery.

"God is love,"
is written upon every
opening bud,
upon the petals of
every flower and
upon every spire
of grass.

Though the curse of sin
has caused the earth
to bring forth
thorns and thistles,
there are flowers
upon the thistles,
and the thorns are
hidden by the roses.

All things in nature
testify to the tender
fatherly care of our God,
and to His desire to
Make His children happy.

His prohibitions and
injunctions
are not intended merely
to display His authority,
but in all that He does,
He has the well-being
of His children in view.

He does not require them
to give up anything that
it would be for their
best interest to retain.

PP 600

You

Love,
why do you,
haunt me?

Emotions,
ever flowing,
never ending.

Why,
do you,
hold me so?

Feelings,
ever growing,
ever knowing,
you fill me.

Love,
so strong,
you free me,
from what,
I do not know.

Love,
you draw near,
ever so close,
ever in the quietness, of my soul.

William Benedict

We Cannot

We cannot
gather the wind,
nor the shadows.

We cannot
gather today,
nor tomorrow.

We cannot
gather the darkness
nor the light.

We cannot
gather the stillness
nor the night.

We cannot
gather the sights
nor the sounds.

We cannot
gather with our hands,
nor with our eyes.

We cannot
gather
what we are not.

When will we gather,
When we have not.

William Benedict

There Is

There is a bridge
that connects—
is it love.

There is a star
that shines—
is it hope.

There is the shadow
of night—
is it the dawn?

There is the lost
ever to be found.

There is the sorrow
who can fill?

There is only one
is that you?

There was a chance
maybe, has left.

There is always
love never ends.

There is tomorrow
why not today?

There is no end
as life will be
in heaven.

William Benedict

When

A stranger,
not to time,
because there
is my share,
but, will
I use it wisely.

In the morning,
in the evening,
the spare time
in between.

A time to let
my thoughts gather.

A time
I made mistakes
some hard,
to replace.

A time
to make and mend.

A time
of peace and quiet.

A time
to roam and let
my mind roam.

A time
to get hold of,
all the good,
the best to have.

Time the maker
of days.

William Benedict

Please

Watch:
When not looking
What can be seen
Where are the eyes
That do not see.

Wait:
A time that is there
What can we do
When there is time
Moments do not know.

Hold:
When watching fails
What can we do
Where are the hands
That do not hold.

Time:
When not around
What can we gather
Where are the paths
That leave no mark.

Only:
When is it now
What has been then
Where are the ways
That have no trace.

William Benedict

A Fool

The thoughts of a fool,
are sayings,
and empty words.

The banners raised
for none to see,
only to a fool.

He who stands alone,
cheering to an
empty world,
when thinking,
of himself,
and on one,
to share
the emptyness,
that haunts
the night.

Making so sad,
one,
who is a fool,
as he steps,
perhaps,
in, only dreams,
as yet unreal,
that is,
to a world.

William Benedict

Spring

The thought of Spring
comes
in each passing day,
as wind and rain, and their songs,
gathering for Spring.

And in each lightened step,
in the echoes of their
song,
bringing warmth and joy,
in sunbeams all aglow.

And in the songs, of birds
on wings, to journey,
from tree to tree,
from tree to limbs,
they bring,
their voices to be heard.

As shouts across the land,
the voice of Spring,
is heard,
to waken hearts and hands
in joyous glad refrain,
in the song of Spring.

William Benedict

Silence

Silence,
is the night,
the darkness,
the light,
their shadows,
round about.

Silence,
who hears,
as that voice speaks.

Silence,
in the sky,
in the deep,
echoes,
who can hear.

Silence,
the whispers,
of life.

Silence,
unknown,
throughout.

Silence,
a picture,
that cannot
be drawn,
in silence.

As the silence
speaks,
truly as,
the light,
brings light.

William Benedict

To Say

A time,
when strangers,
are more important,
than the little time,
we share.

A time,
when all is well,
with hope and love,
a time to make up.

A time,
we have to sacrifice or lose.

A time,
when I can remember,
what I will do,
what I have done.

A time,
to say,
this is the end,
I have run,
out of time,
to say only,
now is...

Good-bye.

William Benedict

Time

Will time,
erase the beauty
of your face?
Or is it the beauty
within, that makes,
love, so pleasing?

Will time,
cover your faults?
Or is it, in my
weakness, that love,
brings me to this
kind place?

Will time,
make my journey,
pleasant, or will
darkness enshroud,
in unmarked shadows,
making, me faint?

Will time,
harbor my fears?
Or will learning,
and understanding,
deepen love, to substain?

William Benedict

Did Love

Where did love
come from,
from some,
distant time?

Was love warm,
and bright,
that enlightens
a smile?

Was love wrapped,
in the nearness
of each moment?

Was love made
to touch,
and melt,
the heart?

To gather
in night,
and day.

Some moments,
when felt,
in pain,
never to atone.

Hope that brings,
as heart yearns,
blind in depths,
whispering love.

William Benedict

Over

    OVER
    the
    SPECTRUM
    of
    TIME
WHO
    CAN
        GRASP
WHO
    CAN
        FATHOM
    the
    REALITY

Let

Let the flower
of obedience
bloom
down the road
of life.

Let the sunshine
bring
the fragrance
of
each bloom.

With each bloom
to come
with shades
of
wonder.

Filling each bloom,
with power
and beauty
to display.

As the radiance
to ever fill my heart with joy.

William Benedict

Taste

Taste of the fruit
of time,
and plenty.

The fruit
of the land,
of Spring,
and Summer.

The joys,
of day,
the joys
of evening.

So much more,
in Spring,
and Summer.

When we begin to
stop learning,

We begin,
to start dying.

William Benedict

As I

As I walk
the path,
the darkness
covers me.

The moments
yearning,
saying,
to come.

The hush of
the night
speaks.

Will you listen?
Will you hear?

Moments are
breathing
softly
to come.

Oh! listen,
to the night
speak.

As the darkness,
is
shouting.

William Benedict

Who

The voice
of God,

Love

Joy

Peace

Found
and expressed,
in nature.

Like,
the rising sun,

Like,
the moments,
the moments,
of time,

Who can fathom
all there is,
that abounds,
expressions,

Of God's
Power,

Of God's
Love.

William Benedict

Images

The images
of love...
who can fathom,
who can measure,
who can fill with hope?

As love seeks in
a quiet voice.

In the mountains
high,
in the valleys
of life.

The voice
ever so quiet,
yet, ever how strong.

To lift up,
to behold,
love a power
to make strong.

The quietness,
in the day,
in the night,
to fill the earth,
to fill the sky.

Love...
the voice,
that has no bounds,
in your heart.

William Benedict

Such Love . . .

Love is global
beyond the span
of time,
from the smallest,
to the biggest,
beyond reach,
nearer than,
each breath.

Before
beginnings, and
no endings.

The center
of life,
above all
there is,
that exists.

Forever...

Is Love.

William Benedict

To See

The journey
   to see

The journey
   to hear

The journey
   to touch

The journey
   to feel

The journey time
to complete.

William Benedict

The Sun

He who rules
the sun
lite sky,

Will rule
the night
of moonlight
stars.

A glow
to shine
across earth's
face.

To brighten
hearts
of man
each day,

A time
of rest,
A time
of joy.

To know
that there
is peace.

Hidden only,
if we see,
as light,
to brighten,
in each day.

William Benedict

Within

The fire
Branding
In a closeness
That is ever near

From cold and heat
To fear
And tears

Reaching with arms
To hold
The fragrance

Burning with hope
To roam
Marked within

Cast forever
Oh! fire of love

William Benedict

His Hands

Love is a principle,
a principle of life
for God is love.

A government of love,
the only bases
for life,
for His glory,
for His honor,
for His pleasure.

We are precious,
made for His plan,
a new beginning,
a new delight.

The joy of heaven,
this place,
called earth.

The sons of heaven,
sang for great joy,
for what,
God has done.

For all to sing,
for great joy,
for all to see,
what His hands,
have made.

William Benedict

To Be

I want to be
in His Presence,
to see,
to touch,
to feel,
to taste,
of His nearness.

To know,
to be,
to sit
at His feet,
I want to be,
in His Presence,
to share,
of my spiritual
needs.

To see,
to touch,
to feel,
in His Presence.

In my walk,
and in my journey,
let it be in peace,
on this journey.

To see,
to touch,
to feel,
today,
on this heavenly
journey,
of life, each day.

William Benedict

To Wait

Has the window
of life,
been brightened,
by love?

Has love cast
its spell,
of hope,
in return?

Through the darkness,
through the rain,
shadows peeking.

Hope is waiting,
and grant...
more than shadows,
of love, want to be.

Shadows wanting,
to be real,
in wonder,
as I wait,
by the gate.

William Benedict

Wear

In the broad ways
of time,
Wear a smile,

To fit
And clothe to size,
Wear it well,

To know
When to learn
Wear it long,

In the broad ways of time	To gather All to have Wear it soon,	In the broad ways of time
To fit,		Wear a smile,
To know	To hope With a dream, Wear it often,	Wear it well,
To gather		Wear it long,
To hope,	To guide To direct, Wear it timely,	Wear it soon,
To guide,	To love For all Wear it always	Wear it often,
To love,		Wear it timely
To say.	To say, And understand, Wear it today.	Wear it always
		Wear it today.

William Benedict

A Life

A life is to be,
a sense of
purpose.

Whether it be,
in a moment,
or a day.

The human being,
is to be,
a life of
meaning,
with a
purpose.

To have
understanding,
for a purpose,
of what, that
purpose is,
is to have a
fulfillment
to reach,
all that is,
and to gain,
through learning,
growing,
filling life,
each day,
with measures,
of joy.

William Benedict

Light

Let your life
be a
candle holder, light.

Love,
Joy,
Peace.

Let this bouquet,
of flowers
bloom.

Let the sunshine
bring,
the fragrance,
of each
bloom.

With such blooms
to come,
with shades,
of wonder.

Filling each bloom,
with power,
to display.

As the radiance
to ever fill,
my heart,
with
everlasting,
moments.

William Benedict

The Peace

Let the flower
of peace
bloom
down the road
of life.

Let the sunshine
bring
the fragrance
of
each bloom.

With each bloom
to come
with shades
of
wonder.

Filling each bloom
with power
to display.

As the radiance
to
ever fill
my heart
with peace.

William Benedict

Such

Is there
such a thing,

as an unmarked grave,
at summer's end.

That hope,
was negative,
and emptines,
was always empty,
and has no home.

Not even,
in the heart of man.

William Benedict

Winter

In Winter,
I never saw,
a rose bloom.

I never saw,
it grow.

Perhaps,
what
I did see,

Was
barren,
and cold.

William Benedict

Come

Come...

walk with me,
through the shadows,
through the dark,
through the light,
of each day.

Oh, come!

walk with me,
for I fear the night,
for I fear the dark.

Shadows will flee away,
as I hold your hand,
shadows not of fear.

Come...

walk with me,
together,
we will walk,
through the shadows,
of night,
without fear.

William Benedict

Memories

that are made
that are cast
in always
wrapped in days
some in summer
most of all
they last forever.

William Benedict

Always

There is a way to make me happy
that is only you,

There is a way to make sad
that is not to see you,

There is a way to make me care
that is to care for you,

There is a way to make me look
that is to look at you,

There is a way to make me love
that is to love you,

There is a way to make me talk
that is to talk to you,

There is a way to make me cry
that is to cry for you,

There is a way to make me hold
that is to hold you,

There is a way to make me to be
that is to always
to be with you.

William Benedict

Giving

What is life

a leaf
a flower
a flowing river,
the deep breath,
the sky a haven.

Joy wrapped in roses,
the silence of peace.

Footsteps marking time
destiny at hand,
in motions,
beginnings,
and endings.

Hope as a refuge
in a dwelling place.

Receiving
and
giving,

All there is of life

William Benedict

Star

The moments are ribbons
that make you precious
wrapped in care
with love.

Tied to a dream
in ever after
with wonder
a shining star.

William Benedict

Before

The foundation was laid
firm and secure,
before the coming
of man,
but man insists,
all evolve
in due time,
leaving man,
in his folly.

All has been gained
through strides,
and man made,
yet, man has not
all the answers.

In his shortness
of time,
pass on all known,
he gathers
like fools,
a toy of time.

Knowledge was before,
a speck in time,
is man,
what has mankind,
to match,
as the heavens,
untouched by man.

William Benedict

Tears

I said tomorrow,
and the rain,
came,

Footsteps dancing
in the night.

In the night
darkness,
shadows,
reaching.

In tomorrow
marking the
way,
as if shouting,
no one to hear.

Troubling pain,
the night, has
passed away,
in gentle tears.

William Benedict

Life

There was a man

There was a woman

Tell me

How you came

He said

by His Hand

She said

by His Hand

As they talked

For nine months

They said

How life began.

William Benedict

Now When

There is a debt,
that must be paid,
It may take
pain and struggles,
It may take
tears and years.

But it cannot be
left undone.

The words,
the feelings,

It cannot be
left unsaid.

The lonely road
I must take.

In the loneliness,
you are not alone.

The sadness to know,
for this sadness
to fill,
the days that come,
will not be,
days undone,
like what,
that is not worn.

The darkness,
will not be dark,
in the night,
of despair.

When,
I am alone.

William Benedict

A Wish

If I had one wish,
would it be for gold,
to buy for gain,
for self, the gain?

Would it be for health
to keep,
when I am in need,
to keep long life,
to count more days,
in joy and peace?

If I had one wish,
to travel every land,
to see and eat,
to learn,
to gather memories,
knowing than,
all people are the same.

Would that wish be,
to help another,
to lift them up,
to ease the hunger,
giving a guiding hand?

A thought,
not of trouble,
but of love and peace,

To share until the earth,
is covered,
a wish that never dies.

William Benedict

Hush

There is a hush,
in the air,
as snowflakes fall,
as nature listens,
for each flake.

Can you hear,
there is silence,
everywhere,
as gentle snowflakes,
come to rest?

To whiten the earth,
in a brightness,
in the sun,
calming the spirit
of man.

Hush !

Can you hear,
there is silence
in the air,
there is peace,
there is a quietness,
and silent beauty,
to rest?

William Benedict

If

Who knows
the shadows
of time,

Who knows
the measure
of man,

Who knows
there is life,

Who knows
what to know,

Who knows
where I am,

Who knows
how to know,

Who knows
all there is
about life.

William Benedict

How Much

Let it be
that my mind
wanders after you,

Let it be all,
that I ever think
of, is always you,

Let it be
hoping you, to not
want to be apart,

Let it be
when you come, to
the window of my heart,

Let it be
I am overwhelmed
but to let it be,

Let it be
sleepless nights come,
because of you,

Let it be
I can't get you,
out of my mind,

Let it be
when I see you,
I want to be near,

Let it be how much,
I care for you.

William Benedict

Welcome

Welcome
        Sunshine

Welcome
        Love

Welcome
        One

Welcome
        Someone

Welcome
        Daylight

Welcome
        Time

Welcome
        Hours

Welcome
        All

William Benedict

One

I gather not
the wind,
nor the sun,
feeling its presence.

In the vastness,
towards the heavens,
in His presence, alone.

There stands,
the Almighty,
to behold.

And I,
but a speck,
of dust,
ever yearning,
to be one,
with Him.

In the light,
of His love.

William Benedict

Prayer

The Lord is my sheperd;
I will lack nothing.

He lets me lie down in
green pastures,
He restores the strength
of my soul.

He guides me along paths
of righteousness.

Even when I have to walk
through a valley of
frightful shadows facing
death.

I will fear no evil
because You are with me,
Your rod and staff
protect me.

You spread out a banquet
for me in the presence
of my enemies.

You anoint my head with
drops of oil.

My heart overflows with
gratitude.

Your goodness AND MERCY
WILL BE WITH ME EVERY
DAY OF MY LIFE, AND
I will live with you in
your house forever.

Psalm 23

Reasons

Sorrows tell
the road is dark,
with all the wrongs,
the heart that aches.

To rest a moment,
is to cry,
in anger why,
is the night dark.

Had not the way,
not been plain,
to hear a voice in silence claim.

Who stands
to hold the tide,
when all about,
knowing you are there,
looking for reasons while it is dark.

William Benedict

A Spring

I hear a voice,
the voice so sweet,
as I walk,
as words speak.

At the dawn,
the light coming,
as the song of birds,
birds,
they sing.

How glad am I,
it is Spring,
it gladdens my heart,
to want,
to sing,
for I,
to know,
it is Spring,
as heaven shouts and earth sings.

William Benedict

Why

Hope wanders
from time,
to time,
softly,
in my mind.

To bring newness
and things,
what I have not.

Thoughts before,
keeps me,
from getting
lost,
in the old things,
that never change.

Going backwards,
instead of
ahead.

Which leaves,
nothing to
look forward
to.

William Benedict

Lord

Lord,

build me a faith,
that is strong
and lasting.

To keep, should
trials come,
though times,
be tainted,
by pain,
with sorrow.

Help me,
to yield,
to be built up,
when it is dark.

To not bow,
in weakness
or
battles flee,
reaching
into the night.

William Benedict

Fill

Love,
why do you
haunt me,
emotions,
ever flowing
never ending?

Why do you
hold me,
feelings ever growing,
ever knowing,
you fill me?

Love,
so strong,
you free me,
from what,
I do not
know.

Love you,
draw near,
ever so close,
in the quietness,
of my soul.

William Benedict

Cover

Cover me black
as the black
of night,
I may be brought,
with feelings,
of regret.
Cover me with love.

Cover me yellow
as the brightness
of the sun,
discarded,
with the fitness,
disrespect.
Cover me with love.

Cover me red
as the blood
of my soul,
running from the
bandishment of fear.
Cover me with love.

Cover me white
where all is, calls
to the standard
as a knight.
Cover me with love.

With all,
may life be true,
with the rainbow
of color,
one day, it will,
be, a life, of love.

William Benedict

Jesus Love

Just like Jesus
I want to be,

Just like Jesus
love,
to cover me.

Just like Jesus
I want to see.

Jesus love,
inside of me.

Just like Jesus
to be filled,
with love,

Just like
Jesus, so you,
may see.

Just like Jesus,
in each day,

Is all I need,
to be like
Jesus.

William Benedict

I Had

I HAD A THOUGHT
AND I lost it,
and I had time,
I thought,
I borrowed.

Time I never
could return,
where both
were found,
in a day.

Time I lost,
along the way,
to barter,
for waste.

While thoughts,
were never
found hidden benath,
like lost treasures,
as if it were,
in the night.

Thoughts hoping,
to be real,
like yesterday.

William Benedict

Since

Love escaped,
and I was saddened,

As hope was low,
making me lonely,

The bright days,
turned into shadows,

As night, I wished,
never came,

Everywhere, I turned,
doubts were many,

And the many dreams,
all have ended,

Wishing tomorrow,
would never come,

Bringing days,
only saddness,

And no one,
to turn to,

Since love,
went away.

William Benedict

I Walk

As I walk the path,
I hear the sounds,
I see the dark,
as I falter in the night.

The anxiety
and stress,
slows my steps,
as weary days,
long for,
tomorrow.

How dark,
how the dark,
has stolen,
my outlook
on life.

Taking me down
the path of
despair,
as the cloudy
lonely days,
dwell,
unfilled.

William Benedict

Choose

Choose today,
not the sorted
suspicion,
nor the darknes
of doubt.

Nor the
waywardness,
of shadows.

But the
waywardness
of one's
ambition,
is to gain,
of one.

Choose not,
selfish ways,
that lead not,
only to self,
destruction.

Why then,
seek,
to destroy all

Man's confidence
his guiding,
strength.

William Benedict

Worry

**WORRY
IS LIKE A
ROCKING CHAIR**

**IT GIVES YOU
SOMETHING
TO DO**

**BUT DOESN'T
GET YOU
ANYWHERE.**

Who Can

Will the shadows
of joy echo,
in the stream
of life.

Will the shadows
of peace,
transcend the calm,
in the beauty,
of each moment.

Shadows that gather,
so softly to speak,
as the stillness,
beckons,
in the silence.

The task of
each moment,
to gather,
to hold,
to be caught up,
in the reality,
the expression of life.

Who can fathom,
that which,
you cannot see?

Who can fathom,
that which,
you cannot hold,
in the moments,
of life?

William Benedict

Will One

When I run out
of patience,
when things,
go wrong,
where, there is
no place to go.

I need to have a
friend.

As the door shuts,
will it be forever,
no room to boast,
lacking all the
frills.

But will I have a
friend.

Who will listen,
even, if I am
wrong.

I cannot find
the answers,
no where to turn.

Will one turn,
to be a
friend?

William Benedict

Plead

Love in
all the windows,
faces every where,
shining
in today,
like the sun's
warm embrace.

Hope is to gather,
thoughts
that often build,
a love to surround,
moments,
passing through.

Love,
kind and tender,
the answer
to our plea.

Strong,
is our plea.

Longing
is our plea.

Longing
now, how to
reach.

William Benedict

Walking

The story,
that never ends,
is like the sun,
that shines.

Shining,
through the day,
and through out always,
to bring all,
that is good,
might I know,
such a story.

To follow the steps,
to the brighter
day,

to always know,
the sun,
out shines,
every cloud.

Lest, I forget,
the better days,
I have been there
but have forgotten
those steps,
I have left behind
and not knowing
the shining path,
I had not seen,
while walking.

William Benedict

A Way

There is a way
to make me happy
that is only you,

There is a way
to make sad
that is not
to see you,

There is a way
to make me care
that is
to care for you,

There is a way
to make me look
that is
to look at you,

There is a way
to make me love
that is
to love you,

There is a way
to make me talk
that is
to talk to you,

There is a way
to make me cry
that is
to cry for you,

There is a way
to make me to be
that is to always
to be with you.

William Benedict

It Matters

Let the presence of love
be present,
It matters.

Let the shadow of love
show,
It matters.

Let the beauty of love
ever shine,
It matters.

Let the stillness of love
visit every moment,
It matters.

Let love be day and night,
It matters.

Let love to be the
burden of your heart,
It matters.

Let love reach far in
the distance of time,
It matters.

Let love always be love
as love will always
to be love.

What matter is love.

William Benedict

Friend

Say
friend!
Have you,
thought of
good today.

Have you thought
to pray.

Has the dawn of
today,
begin to renew
in you.

Has hope guided
this way,
bringing light,
to watch
your steps.

Has time been,
your friend,
to enjoy,
for time is your
best friend,
to cherish every
day,
to be with you
to have,
no matter when.

William Benedict

Ever

Love,

why do you,
haunt me?

Emotions,

ever flowing,
never ending.

Why,

do you,
hold me so?

Feelings,

ever growing,
ever knowing,
you fill me.

Love,

so strong,
you free me,
from what,
I do not know.

Love,

You draw near,
ever so close,
ever in the quietness,
of my soul.

William Benedict

Valley

Down in the valley
is the river,
and the streams,
flowing enchantly,
while the meadow
sways in glee.

As echoes of beauty
are all about,
in smiling faces,
under the sun.

And in joys,
are these,
in the fleeting
moments.

While birds singing,
as birds do sing,
in brightening
voices,
as one may know.

While whispers,
are heard,
in the silence,
to draw near.

Without words,
for all to see,
as the valley,
is aglow,
in the valley,
of laughing
streams.

William Benedict

Passing

When passing down
the country lane,
not turning back,
from whence, I came,
taking the memories,
knowing life,
will no longer,
be the same.

Taking along,
the quietness,
that keeps me,
and not afraid,
knowing,
life will go on.

And the new faces,
that I meet,
will seem,
like new friends,
that are waiting,
just for me.

The new places, to
venture, and to see,
reminding me, of
secret places,
where before, they
were only dreams.

To all the joys,
from day to day,
that greet me,
hoping, they bring,
new plasant,
memories.

William Benedict

Stop

The stillness
in silence,
speaks,
as the voice
of Spring.

The warmeth
the glow,
around me,
around me
yearns.

Like one that
stands alone,
not one move,
not one effort,
can change,
or stop,
the path
of Nature.

William— Benedict—

Words

Words...
that never
run dry,

Your presence,
your joy,
your nearness.

How can I
explain.

To be filled
in the
moments.

How precious
moments,
that fills,
each day,
with love.

William Benedict

Love

Love
is a stream
that can
never run dry.

Love is eternal
your presence
will not leave.

William Benedict

Be

Be like the wings
that carry
a far

Be like the hope
that brings
us near

Be like the echo
to be heard
in the dark

Be like the life
that has
no end

Be all that
life can be

Be that life.

William Benedict

Getting Old

We hold on to time,
as long as
we can,
when we are
young,
not waiting,
to grow up.

Exciting in every
way,
some of the things,
we like to keep.

But they seem to
slip away,
left only
to dream.

For new things,
then suddenly,
we awake,
as time telling
we are getting, old.

William Benedict

Since

Love escaped,
and I was saddened,

As hope was low,
making me lonely,

The bright days,
turned into shadows,

As night, I wished,
never came,

Everywhere, I turned,
doubts were many,

And the many dreams,
all have ended,

Wishing tomorrow,
would never come,

Bringing days,
only saddness,

And no one,
to turn to,

Since love,
went away.

William Benedict

Joy

As I waited,
there was not,
a whisper,
not a call,
yet, I knew.

You were alone,
why not a word
to let me know

How time does pass.

Today, perhaps,
I will know.

As I look into
your eyes,
and see,
your smile,
your
presence
of joy.

William Benedict

Lord

Lord,
build me a faith,
that is strong
and lasting.

To keep, should
trials come,
though times,
be tainted,
by pain,
with sorrow.

Help me,
to yield,
to be built up,
when it is dark.

To not bow,
in weakness
or
battles flee,
reaching
into the night.

William Benedict

Is On

Life is on a journey,
in each day,
in what we do,
in what we say.

In each moment,
in a word in a smile,
in the thoughts,
that reach out.

As life is,
found in the
fulfillment,
of our dreams,
for all the
seasons, of
life, as we
live.

William Benedict

Hear

I never heard,
an ant
speak.

I never heard,
a spider
walk.

Perhaps,
what I did
hear,

was silence,
in the dark.

William Benedict

Why

Hope wanders
from time,
to time,
softly,
in my mind.
To bring newness,
and things
what I haven't.

Thoughts before,
keeps me,
from getting
lost,
in the old things,
that never change.

Going backwards,
instead of
ahead.

Which leaves,
nothing to
look forward
to.

William Benedict

How Much

Night came,
I should have
stopped waiting,

And yet,
does hope,
give up,

Does time end,
the longings,
that are needed,
to show,
that you care.

William Benedict

Moments

The moments are ribbons
that make you precious
wrapped in care
with love.

Tied to a dream
in ever after
with wonder
a shining star.

William Benedict

Destiny

Withal you came,
night owls dreams,
fancy and views
with darkness,
sadness,
faces and fields,
race the seasons.

Bringing hope,
spell bound,
the reasons.

Withal you came,
to beckon me,
reaching,
destiny
reaching,
for yesterday,
as I was in
today,
seeking.

William Benedict

A Friend

A friend is one
That knows me not
Yet a smile beckons

We gather around
Pleasant words
Exchanging thoughts
To hold

A gentleness inviting
Reaching out
To grasp
The kindness

Knowing life has a place
For you
To brighten
My days
Always

William Benedict

The Love Encounter

You meeting me
And our lives met
How you touch me
To such depths
You reach me in all
the days
Our lives will never
be the same
How me long to be near
To think love might
pass away
But often we passing
Through our minds
To each other

William Benedict

Depths of Love

In the depths
I have been moved
By your presence
I have been
Overcome
And undone
By love

I have lost control
of time
Whether it be
Day or night
Come about
By love

I have been overtaken
You welling up within
Just at the thought
of you
Hopelessly
By love

William Benedict

Prisoner of Love

I am a prisoner of love
   That will not let me go
Locked within me
   Is your kindness that haunts
   me so
I cannot escape from the joy
   You hold within me
Marking the time you I behold
   Whence cometh the night
In the bars of your eyes
   That keep me in your love
Released from sorrow and the pain
   In the shadows of your love
   I remain
Imprisoned by you in time
   Totally in love
   Totally blind
I am your prisoner in my mind

William Benedict

In Uncertain Times

Oh! that my heart
      may abound in love,
To escape the fear,
To be not afraid,
      Of the uncertainity,

Oh! that I may see,
      That life,
           Is an adventure,

And that I am
      Of a creation
           To behold,
In the hands of time,

To know
    I have been embraced,
With the kindness
      of life,
        Over shadowing
My understanding,
In that specialness
      Today.

The American Poet

This Is My Life

There is a time,
There is a place,
Where I will be,
When I am born,
Hoping to be loved,
Hoping to be cared for,
To understand
In each day,

Life is one of learning,
Learning to enjoy,
To may be have very little,
Of what life has
To offer,

But to learn
Is all mine to know,
To learn all I can,
To be satisfied,
To know perhaps
A little more each day,
And knowing more along the way,
To be happy where I am,
With all that is free,
To behold the season,
This life,
That has been given
To me.

The American Poet

Remember

If I could only remember,
I am one of a kind.
There is no one quite like me,
And the choice,
I can make
To do with my life,
To be in control,
And not let
Circumstances
Influences
Conditions
And surroundings
Take over my life,
Or control me.

But to know how,
To make the right choices,
About what to do.
And about what to say,
To be the person,
To make for a better life,
And for a belter place,
For myself,
And all I may meet,
To love,
And be warm and kind,
To recognize.
Everyone is looking
For the same,
Knowing, we are all seeking,

This happiness in our time,
Throughout our lives,
And knowing life,
Is not just,
A game of chance.

The American Poet

In The Presence Of Time

As I stood in time.
The presence enveloped
my being,
Enthralled my gaze,
And I was spirited.

I was moved
By the peace and gentleness,
I was held captivated,
In this place of serenity,
Where time spoke,
In the freshness
of each breath.

While the sun in harmony,
Spoke of the warmth and glow,
As the radiant light
cast its spell,
In the essence of it all,

As I stood in the splendor,
In the majesty of nature,
While being held spellbound,
By the wonder of it all,

As nature spoke,
Of the landmark
Of the living,

As time spoke,
In the presence
Of my being.

The American Poet

The Legend

Come experience
The Legend...
The Legend
Of The American Poet,
Experience
The insights
and visions,
Gaze at the tranquility
and beauty.

Come visit the reality,
The facets of the
living,
Bathe in each breath
The supreme moments,
Now in the present.

Come,
Let us visit
in each day,
To know,
And to understand,
To see the marks,
The places,
Fulfilling our lives.

The American Poet

By The River

Often
I come to the river,
And wonder why,

Often
To watch the tide,
Asking
Which is better,
The coming
Or the goings,
And I wonder how,
As I stood by the river,
And watched the tide,
As if being carried away or drifting by,
Life is full of motions
And notions,
And I wonder why,
A better place,
A better time,
And I wonder when,

So often,
I come to the river,
To watch the tide,
Often wondering
Where am I,
Often wondering
Where I am.

The American Poet

Have You Heard Spring Come

Have you heard,
    The whispers of Spring,
  Of the growing grass
      And the sunny beams,
Have you heard,
    The bright yellows speak,
Have you heard Springtime come,
    Come on a path not worn,
      Not in words,
      And not in thoughts,
    Not even an old whisper
        Yielding old roads,
Have you stood by
    The laughing stream,
    And the babbling brook,
Have you heard...
      Even one sour note,
Have you heard
    Spring at all,
Have you heard
      Spring at all,
Wondering
        Where you fit in,
  As just thinking...
Perhaps,
      just to listen,
As someone may have something
    To say,
Perhaps even,
    To say it like Spring.

The American Poet

Counting The Gain

Was I born
To live or die,
Or born to raise
The hearts of man,
Was I born to understand,
And born to raise
The standard high.
In the trials of some days,
Some weary nights,
And days of gloom.

Was I born
To claim all these,
The darkened path
of unsure ways,
And weary footsteps
To often follow,
But will I know
Is it all in vain.
This shell I have made,
Is it to harbor In selfishness,
If only thinking To only pity.

Was I born
To live like this,
Or was I born
To pass through some,
While counting the lost
For gain.

The American Poet

The Path Today

As I walk the path today,
It is not alone,
A face in every flower and tree,
A face of love and care,
A step of faith in shadows,
To guard from Darkened ways,
Sometimes needing
Just to pray,
And be watching and obey,
To hear His words
Of joy so near,
He is always there,
When to listen,
And to wait
So His footsteps
I can trace.

William- Benedict-

Steps Today

Lord,
Guard my steps today,
From the waywardness,
Of fear and anxiety,
From these steps
That may bid me to take,
Show me the path that leads,
To protect
From needless pain,
And as each door opens
Before me,
May the door be one
Of joy and peace,
To strengthen
My faltering doubts,
May I grasp each moment,
And cling
To the lasting parts,
May my eyes see the present
In the shinning light,
To brighten my vision of hope
As onward I go,
May the sunlight ever brighten,
In the presence of this day,
Hoping to look about
And see the realms of joy,
And the lasting peace.

William Benedict

Freedom Nine-Eleven

The very fiber and fabric
Of America
Is woven in our very existence
As the stars and stripes
Of freedom.

The wings of freedom
Mount every face
Of our being
And to all who encompass
What freedom brings.

As on Nine-Eleven
Freedom showed it's face
And shows
What we believe
For we are all one
In spite of our differences
Marching
To freedom's song.

No matter the sacrifice
Should we have to endure
And should we
Have to count the cost
The sacrifice only justifies
The price freely given
For our freedoms.

William Benedict

If Only

If only I could
Keep the moments,
That surround each joy,

If I could only
Keep each day,
The meaning of life,
That holds me close,

To frame those picture
of endless love,
And thoughts that live,
As hope draws near,

If only today
Were tomorrow,
And time would not erase,

If only tomorrow
Were forever,
and time only a place.

William Benedict

Taste and See

Taste of His goodness
His strength, and power,
To build, to uphold,
Taste of His wealth.

Taste of His kindness,
That spreads sunshine and rain,
That melts the hardness,
And consumes the hate.

Taste and see,
That He is good,
For the beauty that grows inwardly
My eyes to see outwardly.

Taste of the good things,
He has prepared,
Gathered and spread,
All over the earth.

Come, and see...what He has made,
From the dust of the earth,
From just...
One piece of clay.

The American Poet

A Place In Time

I dwell in a place called now,
Moved about by time,
The canopy of space
Marks the reverence of each day,
Nature
The temple
of a resting place,
Where the footsteps of God
Trace every breath,
Where the strengths and power
Arrayed in every fashion,
The host of love
Define as peace,
Spread about in the halls
Of taste and see.

I dwell in a place
That is supreme,
I dwell in hope
That still remains
I dwell in life
That is to be,
I dwell in a place
For time to keep,
I dwell with the voices
My heart obeys,
For it is He that speaks.

The American Poet

Spring

It is dawn
It is Spring,
The birds welcoming
The infancy of a new day,
With song,
Dispelling the darkness
In glad refrain,
Awaking to joys
Of another day,
Lifting thoughts,
Lifting the ecstasy
Of the rebirth,
Where hope arises
In the human heart,
And Nature
A living part.

The American Poet

Oh Spring

Whisper to me
Gentle Spring,
In tenderness
And tenderly.
With rays of gold
To light my way.
To brighten
This lonely face.

Bring the freshness
Of my wears,
As fresh as spring
And some kind thoughts,
To lift the darkness
From my soul,
To know that
Life is real.

Oh Spring
So near,
Where is
Your whisperings
The call you bring
The dawn birds sing,
And happy moments
Flowers brim,

Oh where,
Is your cloth so neat,
Bringing joys that cling.

The American Poet

I Sing

While walking
Through the woods,
One day,
A bird was singing
A happy song,
I understood the music,
But I didn't understand
The words.

The gentle breeze
Had a tune,
A tune I knew.
Quite well.
So I paused,
To listen,
To listen,
To the words,
Words that were so clear,
Bringing peace and joy,
Which was all about.
While being there
That day.

I wish I had a song
To sing,
A song they knew,
Quite well,
To sing the words,
To play it's tune,
So they would know,
I sing.

The American Poet

The Stillness

In the stillness...
In the stillness
There is peace,
There the quietness,
This voice that speaks,
That speaks of peace,
Bringing,
To the room of life
To fill.
As this place of peace,
Takes me there,
Willing if I will,
Peace that draws each one
Each day,
Each one that will,
To that quietness
To that peace,
The stillness beckons,
In that wholeness,
To be complete,
To fashion
This peace.
To dress
This face,
To be ...
At peace,
As the stillness whispers.

The American Poet

Freedom's March

We raise our banner
High for freedom,

In Desert Storm
the stripes forever,
In mankind
is freedom's voice,

To be heard
Above Oppression,
For the battle is,
To resist,
To let freedom ring

From the Strong,
to the weak,

The Victor's Song,
Let Freedom ring

Let freedom ring.

William Benedict

Thankful

I'm thankful
for the breath of life
the sunshine and the rain,
Thankful for each day that comes
and all that they bring,
For every tree
and plant that grows
where birds seem to play
Thankful for the day and night
for eyes that can see,
I'm thankful for hands and feet.
to walk and to hold,
Thankful for the things to do
to help along the way,
I'm thankful just to be alive
to see all that is living,
To be a part of all there is
to be a part of giving,
I'm thankful
for health and friends
that, makes life worth living,
For all the joys
and all the cares
Thankful and forgiving,
I'm thankful
for sunrise
and sunsets,
To know
that I have been there,
Thankful to be here,
to dwell

where there is peace,
I'm thankful
To know each day somewhere,
Life is just beginning,
To be a part of all there is,
To be a part Of thé living.

William- Benedict.

A Place in Time

Some stand tall
and some alone,
Shadows linger
where none follow,

He who marvels
wanting hope.
Many stand
where many roam,

Doubts have risen
others fall,
The flight of echoes
how few, how strong,

This stature,
This resolve,
The command
In this fortress
of time,

Only the gallant.
Only the strong,
Claiming this opulent
place,
With high regard and
triuphant,

He stands tall,
Who stands alone,
In the hands
of unknown realms.

William Benedict

TEACH Services, Inc.
P U B L I S H I N G

We invite you to view the complete
selection of titles we publish at:
www.TEACHServices.com

We encourage you to write us
with your thoughts about this,
or any other book we publish at:
info@TEACHServices.com

TEACH Services' titles may be purchased in
bulk quantities for educational, fund-raising,
business, or promotional use.
bulksales@TEACHServices.com

Finally, if you are interested in seeing
your own book in print, please contact us at:
publishing@TEACHServices.com

We are happy to review your manuscript at no charge.

www.ingramcontent.com/pod-product-compliance
Lightning Source LLC
Chambersburg PA
CBHW071217160426
43196CB00012B/2337